STRUCTURES AND TRENDS IN THE GREENING OF INDUSTRIAL RELATIONS IN THE COUNTRIES OF THE EC

EF/92/26/EN

STRUCTURES AND TRENDS IN THE GREENING OF INDUSTRIAL RELATIONS IN THE COUNTRIES OF THE EC

Eckart Hildebrandt
Berlin Science Centre
July 1992

European Foundation
for the Improvement of Living and Working Conditions,
Loughlinstown House, Shankill, Co. Dublin, Ireland
Tel: (353-1) 282 68 88 Telex: 30726 EURF EI
Fax: (353-1) 282 64 56

Cataloguing data can be found at the end of this publication

Luxembourg: Office for Official Publications of the European Communities, 1992

ISBN 92-826-4958-X

© European Foundation for the Improvement of Living and Working Conditions, 1992

For rights of translation or reproduction, applications should be made to the Director, European Foundation for the Improvement of Living and Working Conditions, Loughlinstown House, Shankill, Co. Dublin, Ireland.

Printed in Ireland

Foreword

The following is the second research report of the European Foundation and the Hans-Böckler Foundation in Dusseldorf on the "greening" of industrial relations in the countries of the European Community. The central theme of this project is to investigate what contribution can be made by the system of industrial relations and its principal agents (on the one hand, employers' associations, companies and managers, and on the other, the unions, works councils and employees) to prevent or reduce serious ecological problems. This question is now being examined with increasing attention by the European Community as well; its Fifth Action Programme concerning Environmental Protection expressly underlines the importance of individual companies and employees in effectively protecting the environment.

The primary aim of the two foundations has been to gather empirically well-founded material on the various subjects and the regulation of environmental problems in business and industry throughout Europe, to publicise the industrial relations procedures and strategies they have brought to light and then to discuss them in a supranational context, adding some good examples as a basis for discussion at European level of environmental policy.

This second phase of research has involved commissioning ten national reports and seven case studies. The national reports cover nine countries of the European Community and Austria. The present report provides an initial summary of individual results from the ten national reports, which are themselves to be published in early 1993. The summing up and comparison of results is scheduled for the Summer of 1993.

Dublin and Dusseldorf   September 1992
Dr. Hubert Krieger   Norbert Kluge
European Foundation   Hans-Böckler Foundation

The following paper is an attempt to find an initial answer to the question of whether and, if so, to what extent national industrial relations in the countries of the EC can make an independent contribution to the prevention or reduction of severe ecological problems. At first glance, the answer would appear to be 'No', for the following reasons:
- the institutions of industrial relations are not expressly included in existing national environmental legislation and in the environmental directives of the EC;
- conversely, the laws and regulations governing industrial relations in the individual Member States make no mention of the "environment" as yet;
- many employers' associations and unions have refused, so far, to recognise direct responsibility for environmental policy in any wider sense;
- in practice, among the majority of firms, environmental policy (if it exists at all) takes the form of follow-up environmental protection of a technical nature, provided by departments not specially qualified for the purpose.

For at least two reasons, however, 'No' is not the complete answer.
1. Environment policy at both national and EC level now centres to an ever-increasing extent on the "polluter-pays principle" and the "principle of subsidiarity", which means that the control of environmental risk and damage is being increasingly referred to industry level and to the individual firm (i.e. re-internalised). The EC Environment Commissioner has also recognised that, although environmental policy is now of primary importance in the Community and more than 200 laws have been enacted in connection with the environment, these measures "have only slowed down adverse trends, without actually reversing them." The Fifth Environmental Programme of March 1992 finds that it is becoming increasingly difficult to get by with laws and regulations, that their implementation in

practice is extremely hard to supervise and that greater emphasis is therefore being placed on dialogue, on the inclusion of all social groupings in the responsibility for environmental policy. Under this programme, environmental policy goals and measures are to be defined in a form of concerted action involving all the social partners and groupings. (Commission of the European Communities, Towards Sustainability, March 1992)

2. Secondly, there are many practical examples to show that the parties to industrial relations, in other words the organisations, especially managements and unions, are now confronted to an increasing degree with the ecological consequences of their commercial activities, namely statutory regulations, the cost of raw materials, of energy and of waste disposal, more stringent consumer requirements, consumer boycotting, conflict with residents over noxious emissions and increasingly heavy traffic and the causes of conflicts over health at the workplace. Not only does this lead to loss of legitimate image, it also involves rising costs which are difficult to calculate and often intangible. As a result, we can now observe, in many sectors of the economy, the emergence of an ad hoc and unstructured approach to ecology, from the bottom up and consolidating into a general trend of which very little notice has yet been taken.

The *role of industrial relations* in the development of the European Community's environment policy represents a highly complex process, blending together two radically new developments:

1. A new awareness of ecological problems at industrial relations level, involving very different views of the extent to which the parties and the institutions involved are responsible for environmental matters and the way these are to be handled;

2. The internationalisation of regional policies, especially through the accomplishment of the Single European Market,

in other words the overlaying of traditional, national regulatory systems with new, multinational regulations (in the area of environmental and labour policy, for instance). Both processes are fundamental, as yet largely undetermined in their effect and so remain, within limits, to be influenced by the various social groupings.

With a view to estimating development trends and the scope for formative action in this field, a network of research scientists was set up towards the end of 1990 with the financial support of the European Foundation, the Hans-Böckler Foundation and the Friedrich-Ebert Foundation. National reports on the state of industrial relations and environmental policy have since been produced in ten countries, along with seven case studies on exemplary new developments (see interim report by Eckart Hildebrandt, Industrial Relations and the Environment in Europe, HBS 1991).

The research programme is based on the hypotheses that:
a. in principle, environmental policy in the EC is pursued in two different ways, from the bottom up (pioneering) and from the top down (diffusion).
b. In both situations, the corporate level plays a central part, firstly as a source of innovation and secondly as a site for implementation in practice.
c. To date, innovation and implementation within the framework of industrial relations have not been included as relevant components of national and transnational legislation, they operate at a lower, or at an adjacent level.

So this phase of the project concentrates primarily on the non-statutory, national potential of industrial relations in the context of environmental policy not only at national, but also at EC level. The large number of conferences, programmes, campaigns and committees set up by various national associations, shows that the period of latency vis-a-vis environmental policy has now come to an end for those involved in industrial relations. But despite all this, the dominant forms of policy are still reactive, selective and protectionist. Also prevalent are the delegation of responsibility to the state and the exclusion of industrial relations.

We have used the following explanatory factors in characterising *environmental policy in any country* (borrowing from Jänicke, 1990)(fig. 1):
The last three factors are of particular importance in our own connection, namely the innovative, strategic and consensual ability of the parties to industrial relations.
To begin with, let us also take a brief look at the remaining factors to get an impression of how they differ and what they have in common. The intrinsic difficulties of international comparison have to be taken into account, in other words the different informative value of the indicators selected as a function of conditions in the different countries. On top of this, any national indicator necessarily conceals major differences between regions, between large and small scale enterprises and within associations in individual countries. As a result, the following study is hardly a comparison in quantitative terms, it concentrates more on comparing policies, strategies and regulations, attempting to identify development trends and differences in standards.

I. The Pressure of Political Problems

This paper has little to say on the pressure of ecological problems in the various countries, comparisons are only to be found between individual groups of substances, in the various media, without really discovering any genuine scale of comparison in the process.

However, one indicator we can use is the current, important subject of environmental debate in the individual countries, where the main themes throughout are:

- Traffic,
- Waste,
- Energy and certain hazardous substances (asbestos, PVC, CFCs, etc.).

Fortunately, there is some body of data on *environmental awareness* which reveals the following set of circumstances (fig. 2):

- Every one of the survey countries revealed a very considerable need for action. This finding itself conceals differences which can be explained by various different factors.
- Great need for action is expressed in countries with a comparatively high level of pollution and a comparatively low level of environmental protection (Greece, Italy and Spain). Conversely, countries with a relatively high level of protection express a below-average need for action.

Looking at dissatisfaction in a somewhat different light, under the heading of such individual environmental components as drinking water, noise, air pollution, etc., there are considerable differences in the level of dissatisfaction with individual areas of pollution. But it is worth noting, on the other hand, that individual countries have their own consistent levels of dissatisfaction in all fields. For instance, dissatisfaction is greatest in almost every field in Greece, while in Denmark, it is lowest. This would also indicate that there does not seem to be any strikingly different emphasis on particular problems in particular countries.

This different perception of the subject has its inverse analogy in the *membership of environmental organisations* as an indicator of the strength of national environmental movements. While membership is very high in Denmark and the Netherlands, it is lowest in Spain and Greece. In the first group of countries, pressure for high environmental standards already appears to have been put into practice in organising and institutionalising the protective interest, which itself has led to a relatively high level of satisfaction.

II. Capacity to deal with Problems

II.1 Economic Potential
The data on economic potential, measured by per capita BIP, tends to reveal three separate groupings, namely a leading group comprising Denmark and the Federal Republic of Germany, a wide middle group which includes France, the Netherlands, Belgium, Italy and Great Britain, then a weaker group composed of Spain and Greece. This classification is based both on environment-protection potential and on above-average environmental stress attributable to the level of economic activity and prosperity (energy consumption, number of cars per head of population).

II.2 Economic Potential of Environmental Policy
The disparity between EC countries increases substantially in the specialised economic sector of environmental technology, undoubtedly one of the most important sectors of future growth. Germany takes a clear lead in terms of state expenditure on R&D, the number of environmental protection patents and the size of the environmental protection market, followed at some distance by France and Great Britain. The potential under these headings still remains barely developed in Spain and especially in Greece, from which it may be assumed that the economic background for the greening of corporate policy is probably at its weakest in these countries (fig. 3).

II.3 Development and Effectiveness of National Standards and Regulatory Systems
In analysing basic legal conditions, we need to look at two legal systems which have seen very little association with one another to date, namely the different *employment systems* of individual countries and their environmental legislation.
The essential aspect of *environmental protection* is seen as a

body of regulations covering:
- Emissions,
- Air purity,
- Water protection,
- Protection of human health against environmental hazard
- Protection of natural resources.

Countries differ essentially in their existing regulations and the legal reality of these and in the degree to which environmental law is fragmented or harmonious. Important indicators in this context are the existence of a ministry for the environment and associated department of the environment, as also the introduction of a uniform environmental protection act (take for example the Environment Protection Act of 1990 in Great Britain and of 1991 in Denmark).

EC Directives play an important part in the process of assimilation, although their adoption itself gives rise to a different set of problems. They are considered to be of relatively little importance in the Netherlands, even sometimes in France and Germany as well, since as a rule the level of protection in these countries may already be higher. There is a strongly defensive reaction in Great Britain, for conceptual reasons more than anything else, though from the opposite viewpoint, the adoption of EC Directives is seen as one of the most important ways of raising the level of protection in Great Britain. The weaker group of countries is dominated by restrictive national conditions and major problems with implementation.

Moreover, virtually every country introduces its own particular conditions and restrictions in given problem situations (e.g. organic solvents in Denmark, or the quality of drinking water in Great Britain).

III. Links between Environmental Policy and Industrial Relations

III.1 Statutory Regulations

Of central importance to our own enquiry is the *link between these two regulatory systems*, in other words the extent, if any, to which the parties and institutions of industrial relations are involved in the implementation of environmental legislation. The question is, then, to find how the responsibilities and supervisory rights stipulated by law are allocated within the individual firm and factory. These may take the following forms:

- The constitution of an independent, specialised responsibility alongside the departments concerned (statutory and voluntary company officer),
- Definition of specific, personally assigned responsibility for corporate policy at board level,
- The establishment of specific, specialised departments (often in conjunction with worker protection),
- Involvement of employee representatives in varying ways in the implementation and supervision of environmental legislation (joint committees, for example).

Progress is slow under this heading. Austrian and German company-related environmental legislation envisages the appointment of an independent "environmental officer"; a Brussels Region agreement on an "eco-conseiller" within the company has just miscarried.

The appointment of a person responsible for environmental matters at company management level is known to me only from the amended version of the Federal Republic of Germany's Federal Anti-Emissions Act, passed in the Autumn of 1990. However, a few of the national reports mention that responsibility of this kind is initiated by some large companies on a voluntary basis.

All told, then, statutory access by employee representatives to the executive and supervisory rights provided in environmental protection regulations is virtually non-existent at immediate company level. Some German environmental laws provide minimal rights of access to company officers.

The surveys have also shown that, contrary to a central theme of scientific discussion, there is no tendency to move from central to decentralised regulation. But for a few variations, environmental policy remains predominantly a matter for centralised regulation (this is especially so in France). A trend towards decentralisation was found only in Italy, while in Austria there is a move towards more central control by the state. But there is an important *trend towards voluntary agreements between the state and industrial organisations*, as expressed for example in the Netherlands government's National Environmental Policy Plan (NEPP), which places the main emphasis of state environmental policy on voluntary agreements with the employer associations. While this development is reflected in all countries except Great Britain and Greece, actual commitment on the part of companies and employer associations is regarded as rather a rarity in the majority of countries (D, A, UK, E, G), more often found in the Netherlands as part of the Company Environmental Protection System, in Italy (especially in the chemical, energy and metal industries) and also in Germany.

III.2 Indirect Access to Environmental Protection

Indirect access by employee representatives and unions is made under various headings:
- protection of health and safety at work;
- securing of employment;
- working conditions, humanising of labour;
- quality of life;
- consumer interests.

Access to the protection of health and safety at work is clearly a dominant feature in all reporting countries. All of them have laws that provide for company committees and officers involving representation of employee interests:

"In the Federal Republic of Germany, in Luxembourg, in Italy and in the Netherlands, the works councils elected by employees have differing functions and rights in respect of the protection of health and safety at work, including the right to accept or reject measures proposed by the employer, be involved in planning, supervise the compliance of particular measures with statutory regulations, obtain relevant information and accompany and consult with factory inspectors on their visits.

"Belgium prescribes a special committee for consultation between employer and staff in all companies of more than 50 employees, while in France and Portugal the law prescribes a health and safety committee in all enterprises or firms with more than 50 employees. Committees of this kind are also required in Spain as a function of the number of employees and the nature of risk.

"In Denmark and the United Kingdom, it is a requirement for employee representatives with safety duties to be elected by the employees. These representatives are members of the works safety committee and are entitled to obtain all relevant information and consult with the competent factory inspectorates.

"In Spain, Greece and Ireland, consultation is not legally stipulated to the extent described above."
(Social Europe 2/90, 37)

Almost every country is now endeavouring to extend the authority of the Health & Safety Officer and the H & S Committee to include environmental aspects, a most obvious requirement in connection with hazardous substances and chemicals. An attempt is being made to bring about this broader responsibility through legislation, though also through voluntary agreements. The varying degrees of effort employed by individual countries to arrive at a wider, pragmatic interpretation of H & S authority have met with no more than very limited success and, in fact, have clearly revealed the need for official reform (see fig. 4). Our survey reveals that all responding countries (with the exception of Great Britain) look on statutory requirements and regulations as the principal and most important form of control.

III.3 Independent Activities by the Associations

As we have seen, the involvement of industrial relations institutions in the implementation of environmental legislation is very much in its infancy and its progress is very slow. Union initiatives to extend their rights in this direction have already broken down or come to a standstill on many occasions.

Accordingly, the growing pressure that this problem exerts on business and industry is more forcefully dealt with by *independent activities* at association, company or factory level.

We found environmental programmes and individual management posts among national employer associations and unions in almost all the countries surveyed (with the exception of Greece). One of the most highly developed systems appears to exist in Italy, in the Industrial Environment Association of the CONFINDUSTRIA, a separate institute with its own journal and series of conferences, then on the other side, the joint "Programme of Work" of the various unions, the CISL, UIL and CGIL. We have hardly any information on the spread of such programmes and campaigns to individual associations and firms, but it is probably very limited, as the umbrella associations are generally unable to put their members under obligation.

The scene at industrial and especially at company level is dominated by a large number of individual initiatives under the banner of a general profession of responsibility for the environment. There seems to be a considerable gap between the various countries in terms of the variety and number of these initiatives, with only a few examples to be found in Spain and Greece so far. As a rule, a number of (international) large companies, the chemical, metal and cement industries, and the public service take pride of place. From the union viewpoint, the scope for organisation at company level is necessarily more limited, being restricted to the emergence of individual specialists. The institution of staff working groups or the conduct of works campaigns (relating to pollutants or waste collection, for instance) are even more rarely encountered.

One substantial reason for the independent and differing approach of these two sides of industrial relations is undoubtedly the *different motives behind their activities*. For the most part, entrepreneurs react to new laws and public pressure which is usually closely associated with the environmental movement. The unions, on the other hand, see themselves face to face with their members' changing values, the risk to jobs and new opportunities for employment. The rising cost of industrial pollution and a more demanding body of customers or consumers are beginning to make themselves increasingly felt in those countries with a large-scale environmental market and more stringent environmental legislation.

In keeping with this background of differing motive and different organisational interests, the *basic strategic options* available to the two parties are also different. The most important aspect they share in common, but also the feature that distinguishes them most, is statutory regulation. For both parties, the observance of existing protective law comes first in their commitment to the environment, although this observance itself is often enough disputed. On the other hand, the employers' associations in all the survey countries plead for less intervention by the state, while the unions plead for more. The 'more' they ask for is firstly an expansion and intensification of environmental legislation and secondly the inclusion of union and employee representatives when putting such legislation into practice (information, participation and training). The greatest dividing line between entrepreneur and unions is probably to be found in this second field of participation by law.

III.4 The State of Union Environmental Activities in Selected EC Countries

Without any claim to a full description or direct comparability, the following rough summary taken from the national reports is intended to illustrate the ideas and activities of the trade union associations in the various individual countries.

The situation in *Spain* is described as one of tension between two positions at union management level. On one side, there is a minority of ecologically-minded union officials who have a broad understanding of the environment and attribute the ecological crisis to the capitalist economic system. They seek funds to close particularly harmful industries and promote industries engaged in environmental renewal. They demand a wide-ranging educational campaign and greater union participation in statutory decision-making bodies. The latter demand they share with the more pragmatic members of the union movement who direct most of their attention to health and safety within at work. Union policy vis-à-vis severe environmental pollution by industry is remarkable more by its reserve and its readiness to make concessions.

The *Italian unions* have been relatively late in reacting to the environmental problem, distancing themselves from it and having a very narrow understanding of it. Then, the three major umbrella associations, the CGIL, CISL and UIL, dedicated the years 1989 and 1990 to environmental policy, which ended in a comprehensive programme of work for the unions' environmental department, comprising:
- legislation to regulate the ecological reorganisation of production,
- the implementation of rights to information and training and of safety reports in risk-prone areas of production (the EC's Seveso Directive),
- the application of methods for estimation of environmental consequences,
- the expansion of company-based environmental research,
- the establishment of environmental information systems,
- the conclusion of national and company-based agreements
- the organisation of regional environmental meetings (Adria, Venice).

Cooperation with environmental groups has been built up to an above-average extent and there is also an environmental organisation appropriate to the unions (ambiente e lavoro). A well-defined "emergency management" system, involving local authorities, environmental groups, companies and unions, has evolved to deal with environmental disasters, serious legal infringement, abnormal occurrences, etc. In connection with the verification of EC Directives, the Italian unions are trying in particular to increase citizens' and workers' rights to obtain information and put forward suggestions.

As a characteristic example of the *situation in Greece*, no right whatever to negotiate collectively on matters of health and safety at work existed up to 1990. Although the new Act 1876/90 makes no explicit mention of environmental protection, it is hoped that environmental matters will also be included in future. One basis for this will be the work of the Athens Labour Centre, which prepares analyses and views on environmental problems in cooperation with engineers, chemists, local authorities and development agencies. Their ideas focus mainly on a system of state subsidies for modernising companies and for financing relocation to special industrial zones. Union ideas, however, are still closely bound up with health and safety at the workplace and are characterised by conflicts over job security.

The three major *French unions* set up their own environmental commissions in the early Eighties, although campaigns in the environmental field were then fairly isolated, covering such aspects as nuclear energy, the increased incidence of cancer in the iron and steel industry, compensation for asbestosis and action against the illegal dumping of waste. The enfeeblement of the French unions during the Eighties is regarded as being responsible for some decline in the importance of environmental topics by comparison with others. Generally speaking, the attitude of the CGT is characterised by a policy well-disposed towards industry and directed to growth. It supports industry's technological solutions, even when these are incompatible with the demands of the environmental movement. Demands at company level are related to more environmental authority for the works committees (CHSCT) and better information on health and safety matters for workers and the population at large.

At their congresses in 1990, the *Belgian unions* accorded high status to environmental protection inside and outside the company and passed some fundamental resolutions. The socialist FGTB, for

instance, calls for a general ecological turn-around in economic policy through the general introduction of the preventive principle, the "polluter pays" principle and the principle of price adapted to cost. The main demands of the Belgian unions are directed towards the state. The Christian CSC is looking for:
- the creation, supervision and general introduction of more environmental standards,
- higher taxation of environmentally harmful products and production processes,
- the promotion of "clean technologies",
- improved coordination between the country's three regions
- an offensive environmental policy at EC level.

There were various suggestions with regard to an ecological policy at company level, for instance the extension of the health and safety committee's responsibility to include environmental matters, provision of information for employees and their involvement in dealing with waste, as well as an annual stocktaking of company policy (an audit, as it is called).

Analysing the environmental policy of the *Netherlands unions*, it can be seen that a first phase in which the environment came behind the economy has been followed by a second phase which considered environmental protection and employment to be mutually exclusive to a large degree and delegated sole responsibility to the state and the employer; then, beginning in 1987, this phase was succeeded in its turn by a third one which actively promotes environmental policy. This policy concentrates on the one hand on campaigns for cleaner products and production processes and on the other for an increase in the democratic rights of its members. Measures introduced are far-reaching and include participation in national environmental policy, close cooperation with environmental protection organisations and universities, agreements with employers' associations, the conclusion of collective agreements and campaigns among members. A special feature of the situation in the Netherlands is the support that the unions and environmental organisations give to the progressive idea of the "Company Environmental Protection System", while at the same time demanding a greater obligation to provide information (audits).

In its position as stated in 1990, the *Danish Trade Union Federation*, LO, clearly declared its responsibility for environmentally compatible development and put this into practice in the form of an environmental action plan, following ample debate among the unions. The genuine nature of their concern is indicated by the major importance attached not only to protectionist goals (securing jobs through improvement in competitive position), but also to environmental aspects; for example, the intention to make "environmental watchmen" of Public Service Union and Womens' Union employee representatives, or another union's concentration on a "green life-style". In practical policy terms, for instance, the responsibility of safety departments has been widened in an agreement with the metal industry (IMO Agreement). Binmen are being trained as supervisors of waste disposal in residential areas. The Food Industry Union promotes projects that encourage a healthy diet. Nonetheless, substantial differences still exist between planners at union head office and interests on the shopfloor.

The *Federal German unions* can cite a long tradition in the protection of workers in industry, as well as in the struggle for the working population's quality of life. But despite this, they have for many years taken a critical to disapproving view of the strong upsurge in the environmental movement. Neither in the comprehensive regulations concerning labour-management relations and co-determination, nor in environmental legislation, is there any embodiment of employee-representative responsibility for environmental matters and, so far, any initiatives in that direction have failed.

While the German Trade Union Federation is responsible as the umbrella organisation for the general social aspects of environmental protection, the various industrial unions concentrate on their own industrial problems, such as replacement of harmful substances, environmentally friendly building, a healthy diet, priority for rail traffic, or a green system of procurement in the public service. The employer associations and company managements prefer independent strategies, meaning voluntary commitment vis-à-vis the state and some limited involvement of the works councils (essentially providing rights of information and further education or training). Alongside a growing number of agreements between employers and works councils (though it is only in the chemical industry that these are found consistently), the inclusion of ecological considerations in collective agreements is now an increasingly important matter of discussion. Initiatives of this kind have been somewhat diluted by the economic strain now imposed by the new Federal Lands to the east.

In *Great Britain*, the environmental policy of the umbrella organisation, the TUC, has been given a systematic basis through the foundation of an "Environmental Action Group". This group's first report in 1990 provides a general view of ecological topics, possible union activities and suggestions for the "greening of the workplace". Aspects sought after include:
- wider authority for health and safety officers,
- new employee information, participation and negotiation rights, and
- a national programme of education in environmental protection.

Central importance is attached to the demand for participation in "environmental audits".

The report also includes a package of concrete measures for the individual unions and the drafting of a comprehensive company agreement ("Green Agreement"), to be concluded as far as possible by every company. Undoubtedly, the aggressive stance of the TUC is also attributable to the anti-union policy of the Tory government and represents an attempt to develop a new agenda for itself.

In doing this, the umbrella council places particular emphasis on the cooperative potential of environmental policy.

In summary, it is clear from all the reports that very similar difficulties arise for the unions everywhere in developing an environmental policy. These difficulties can be brought to the common denominator of a very pronounced *diversity of approach to the environment*, including differing degrees of ecological commitment on the part of individual unions, the organisation of highly varied occupational groupings within any one union, different ways of seeing things at national, local and company level, and controversy between a broad understanding of the environment as an aspect of social policy and a narrower understanding based on the classical protection of labour. Added to this is the problem experienced in every country, in specific disputes at company level, of simultaneously protecting the environment and securing jobs. Considering these difficulties of principle and the generally new nature of the environmental topic within the union movement, it is quite understandable that at the moment, many countries should still be directing their principal activities towards mobilising their members and qualifying their officials, beginning, in other words, by creating within their own organisation the necessary conditions for an independent environmental policy. In some countries, like France and Great Britain, the realisation of these conditions is made more difficult by a general weakening in the position of the unions.

III.5 Approaches towards Cooperation

Advances in industrial environmental policy are more to be found in the area of *voluntary, ad hoc cooperation*, with greater importance also being attached to specific national systems of industrial relations which have a historical background. National employment systems stipulate, among other aspects, the principles and the limits of cooperation between management and unions. Basically, the same principles are applied to new fields of interest like environmental policy, even when these include new potential for cooperation. The countries of the EC take up a wide range of positions vis-à-vis industrial cooperation, with a definite concentration on more cooperative options. A rough outline of this kind must of course be broken down to allow for individual industries and arrangements at different levels. Denmark, Belgium, the Netherlands and Italy appear to enjoy considerable cooperation at national or regional association level, sometimes reaching down to the individual company. In Germany, cooperation seems to be more at company and factory level. Another significant factor is the very substantial differences that exist in the binding character and stability of such cooperation.

By way of example, fig. 5 shows some important instances of voluntary cooperation in different countries.

In these examples and also in the case studies, we found some important starting points for an ecologically oriented expansion of industrial relations. It will now be the task of our forthcoming research work to examine the effectiveness, capacity and potential universality of these approaches in greater detail.

On the other hand, examples of this kind can only be amplified and expanded upon if a realistic view is taken of the *limits* to any process of greening industrial relations and if the various obstacles to this process are at the same time removed. The national reports are very much in agreement on this point, universally regarding the *principal obstacle* as being the entirely unsatisfactory level of union or employee-representative involvement in corporate environmental policy, chiefly expressed in the employers' refusal formally to approve this involvement.

A *second* set of obstacles which was also mentioned throughout included the still far too scant attention paid to this new subject, the lack of an infrastructure and the lack of authority enjoyed by both parties.

It is pointed out that both sides are still committed to an ideal of industrial productivity which bars access to any deeper level of ecological thinking.

The countries of southern Europe gave particular mention to a *third set* of obstacles, namely a weak economy, a highly fragmented labour market and a concentration on progress which will bear no criticism (i.e. quantitative growth).

The great difficulty that there is in precisely defining the cooperative potential of industrial relations on environmental matters was demonstrated by the very different answers given in the reports to the question of possible areas of consensus. Some entirely different aspects were touched upon, including ideological solidarity, common economic interest, national employment and social systems, practical examples at company and industrial level, and absence of consensus because of a consistent policy of conflict (Great Britain) or total lack of concern (Greece).

These replies show the complexity of the social consensus process and the impossibility of simply defining it within the context of an environmental policy. Areas of consensus sometimes develop only in the course of a regulatory process, as we have already been able to show in selected case studies on "good practices". Accordingly, it is of crucial importance to initiate and disseminate a process of learning with regard to possible areas of consensus.

IV. Cooperation in Discourse

The Brussels Workshop in November 1991, at which this interim review of the national reports and two case studies were presented, also gave the association representatives the opportunity to take a stance at EC level on the beginnings of this research project and present their own points of view.

them to influence management's mainly compensatory approach based on investment, product development and choice of technology. Environmental protection is a matter for the boss.

The union representatives, in contrast, preferred a broad definition. They also feel responsible for the quality of life and see a close, parallel association between work and the environment, especially under the heading of health. However, such a wide, social-policy based understanding of union responsibility is only shared to a limited extent by the national unions and their members and, taking another view, it does not go far enough to cater effectively for the interests of local residents, for instance.

The social partners accordingly made a case for *broader cooperative relations at industrial and regional level*, in which the various social groupings would be included in accordance with their interests. The need to look for solutions and exert control at higher than individual company level was largely undisputed, even though it would limit the individual firm's or the individual association's room for manoeuvre. This would naturally modify the role of the unions, but there are three very good reasons in favour of their participation: employees are at the same time residents and consumers, they as producers have a share in causing pollution and the routine implementation of corporate environmental action can only be effective and remain under control when the employees are involved. In this context, however, the employers' association called for a distinction between union and employee representation.

As outcome of this general exchange of experience, ways were sought to reduce the gap between awareness of the environment and everyday action within the company. An ambivalent view was taken of the role of the media which, by publicly scandalising them, have been the first to reveal many risks and generate pressure for action. On the one hand, emphasis was placed on the importance of the media as watchdog and exerter of pressure while, on the other, there was criticism of its exaggerating and discrediting effect. Neither was there unanimous approval of the part that science has to play. While all association representatives shared the proposed aim that the specialist sciences should be obliged to provide objective knowledge and standards which could be generally applied to new regulations, there was also the opinion that extensive scientific preoccupation and the attendant publicity would evoke entirely unjustified fears among the general public and change control into chaos.

Two lines of approach were developed as definite points on which to concentrate:

1. The need for more stringent *statutory standards* whose supervision both from outside and within the company would need more resources (or incur penalties).

2. There was a call to find, analyse and propagate exemplary procedures and solutions. Such examples of *good practice* can be extremely convincing. Environmentally active entrepreneurs would need to go on the offensive and also, where necessary, take action against particularly careless or obstinate companies. This could very easily give rise to coalitions composed of environmentally active management and employee representatives in opposition to polluters of the environment.

Taken overall, then, there was lively debate which on some occasions directly addressed the demands made of this project, namely the refining of further case studies on "good practices", more precisely determining, in the process, the opportunities and limits of commitment to the environment. This would also mean the continued investigation of specific and generally applicable instruments of state environmental policy, suitable as means of generating awareness in environmental matters and raising the level of protection.

Addendum: A final report on the project is to be available by the end of 1992; the interim report and the national reports on Belgium, Denmark, Germany, France, Greece, Great Britain, Italy, the Netherlands, Spain and Austria are already obtainable from Dr. Hubert Krieger, the European Foundation for the Improvement of Living and Working Conditions, Loughlinstown House, Shankill, Co. Dublin, Ireland.

Biographical note: Prof. Eckart Hildebrandt, economist, engaged at the Berlin Science Centre since 1977 in the fields of "rationalisation and the policy of the unions", "conversion of armaments" and, since 1989, "ecologically extended labour policy", was appointed Professor of Sociology at the University of Bremen in 1992.

ANNEX 1

W Z B   Ecologically extended Labour Policy Project

I.   THE PRESSURE OF ECOLOGICAL PROBLEMS

(in the realms of water, air, soil, waste, etc.)

II.   THE PRESSURE OF POLITICAL PROBLEMS

- Environmental awareness
- Environmental movement
- Ecological shadings of parties and media

III. CAPACITY TO DEAL WITH THE PROBLEM

- Economic potential
- Development and effectiveness of national standards and regulatory systems
- Economic potential of environmental policy (cost reduction, market development)
- Innovative skills
- Strategic skills
- Consensual capacity

Factors explaining National Environmental Policy   1
(after Jänicke, 1990)

ANNEX 2

W Z B   Ecologically extended Labour Policy Project

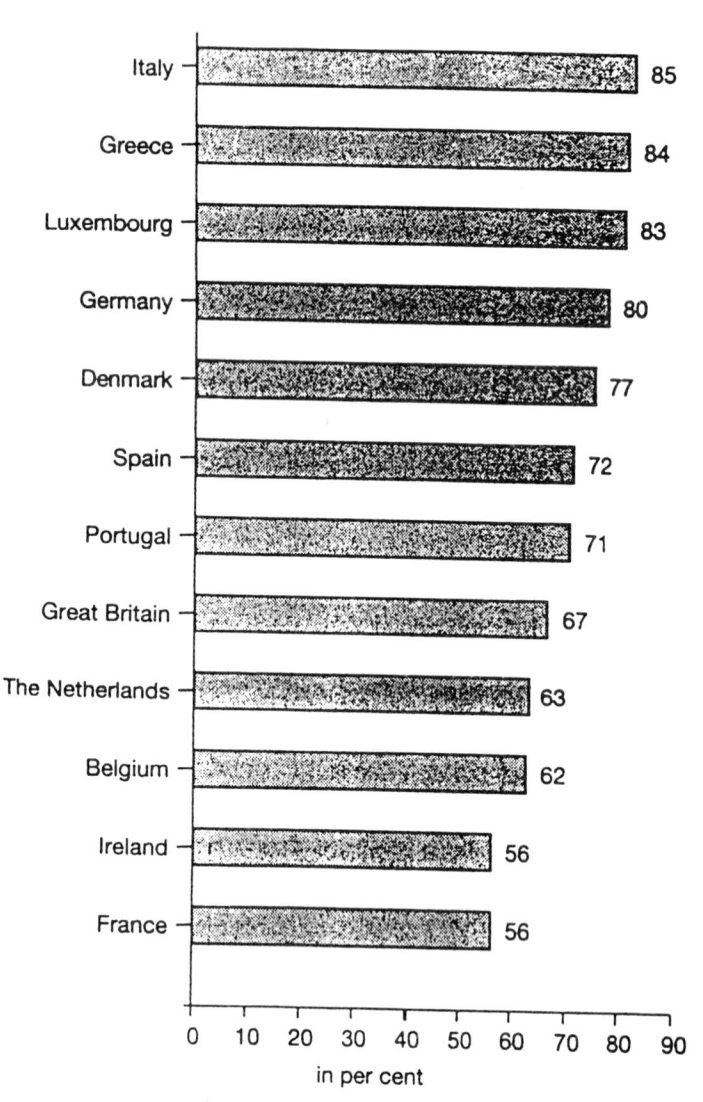

COMPARISON THE IMPORTANCE OF ENVIRONMENTAL
PROTECTION WITHIN THE EC

Seen as an urgent problem requiring immediate action in

The Environment in Public Opinion
(Task Force Report on the Environment and the
Internal Market, Bonn 190, S. 43)

ANNEX 3/1

W Z B   Ecologically extended Labour Policy Project

Environmental Protection Markets, 1987	Environmental Expenditure(1)	
	Value (bn. ECU)	Percentage of of EC Total (%)
EC	39.8	100.0
Belgium	1.2	3.0
Denmark	0.8	2.0
FR Germany	14.5	36.4
Greece	0.2	0.5
Spain	1.2	3.0
France	7.7	19.3
Ireland	0.2	0.5
Italy	4.6	11.6
Luxembourg	0.0	0.0
The Netherlands	2.0	5.0
Portugal	0.1	0.3
United Kingdom	6.8	17.1

(1)   Estimate of national expenditure under the headings of air, water, waste and noise.
(2)   As percentage of total EC expenditure; OECD figures.

Source: Données économiques de l'Environnement - BIPE.

European Environmental Protection Patents, 1986	Total
EC	510
Belgium	3
Denmark	19
FR Germany	309
Greece	0
Spain	16
France	62
Ireland	4
Italy	11
Luxembourg	1
The Netherlands	23
Portugal	0
United Kingdom	62

Economic Potential of Environmental Policy   **3/1**
(Panorama of EC Industry, 1990, pp. 144, 150 and 157)

ANNEX 3/2

State Expenditure on Research and Development in Environmental Protection

(Billion ECU)	1985 Value	Percentage of R&D (%)
Denmark	6.6	1.5
FR Germany	309.3	3.1
Spain	9.2	1.0
France	51.1	0.5
Italy	44.6	1.0
The Netherlands	53.7	4.1
United Kingdom	99.6	1.1
USA	259.5	0.5
Japan	n.a.	n.a.

Source: OECD

Economic Potential of Environmental Policy   3/2
(Panorama of EC Industry, 1990, pp. 144, 150 and 157)

ANNEX 4/1

W Z B   Ecologically extended Labour Policy Project

A   ☐   In the intention of developing public service guidelines, employers' associations and unions are working together with representatives of government on selected environmental questions, in such bodies as the Chemicals Commission and the Environment Foundation.

        ☐   Works council information rights based on the Labour Act and also including environmental aspects; rights of intervention in cases of acute environmental hazard and the right to object to environmentally harmful production processes.

B   ☐   The new regulation concerning the authorisation of environmentally harmful processes in Flanders includes rights of information for works councils and labour safety committees.

        ☐   A Ministry of Labour bill envisages a broadening of the statutory right to information enjoyed by labour safety committees to include environmental matters.

        ☐   A proposal by the Flemish Minister for the Environment aims at concluding a general, tripartite agreement on guidelines for future environmental policy.

        ☐   The Brussels Region has a bill concerning a joint agreement on environment officers at company level.

        ☐   A ministerial campaign regarding environmental audits which are also to be placed at the disposal of labour safety committees.

D   ☐   The Hazardous Substances Order, supplementing the Chemicals Act, includes certain rights to information and consultation for works councils.

        ☐   The German Trade Unions' Federation's (DGB) proposal to have the Labour-Management Relations Act amended, envisaging among other aspects an expansion of works-council rights to include environmental matters, has so far been turned down.

DK   ☐   The Working Environment Act envisages cooperation within a Working Environment Council with tripartite representation.

**Environmental Legislation and Industrial Relations –
Present Situation and Developments**   **4/1**

ANNEX 4/2

W Z B   Ecologically extended Labour Policy Project

I   ☐   A proposal by the parliamentary LAMA Commission envisages the appointment of safety officers.

    ☐   The High Risk Areas Act stipulates the establishment of regional committees comprising representatives of individual companies, the unions and employee interests.

    ☐   A draft agreement between the Ministry for the Environment and the boards of the CGIL, CISL and UIL unions envisages union participation in the development of the new Three Year Environment Programme, in the committees appointed to ecological crisis regions and in the application for projects relating to the latter.

NL   ☐   Article 11 of the Working Environment Act provides that company management must avoid risk to the safety and health of persons in the immediate vicinity of the plant. It is thereby established that environmental matters are the concern of the company and are also part of the work of the employee representatives.

    ☐   The FNV Trade Union Federation is calling for inclusion of environmental protection in the Employees' Representation Act.

UK   ☐   The regulations governing the control of substances harmful to the health (COSHH) stipulate that companies must inform, instruct and further train employees at risk.

    ☐   Since the government's proposal for a comprehensive environmental protection ruling (White Paper) does not envisage any involvement of the unions and workers' representatives, the Labour Party and the TUC have suggested the establishment of environmental committees and information rights for the unions.

**Environmental Legislation and Industrial Relations –
Present Situation and Developments**

ANNEX 5/1

W Z B   Ecologically extended Labour Policy Project

B   ❏   Joint recommendation on environmental information within the chemical industry.

D   ❏   Central agreement on information, consultation and further training of works councils in the chemicals industry; to be followed by more than 40 corresponding company agreements

        ❏   Draft environmental collective agreement for the food industry, produced by the NGG Union

        ❏   Individual company collective agreements (Teldec) and employer/works council agreements (ZF Friedrichshafen) in the metal producing and using industries

        ❏   Isolated joint environmental committees

DK   ❏   Joint position of Danish employers' association and the trade unions' federation on improvement in environmental legislation

        ❏   Negotiations between Ministry for the Environment, business associations and individual unions, dealing with such topics as reducing and recycling PVC

        ❏   Agreement on environmental protection within the metal industries, involving the labour safety committees

G   ❏   First joint discussion of a policy for the "Hellenic Institute for Health and Safety at Work"

I   ❏   Negotiations between the government, the Confindustria employers' association and the unions, to include environmental problems.
Agreement on the establishment of a joint commission to investigate environmental problems in Lombardy

        ❏   National employment agreement in the chemical industry, which includes important environmental policy provisions (concerning environmental officers, environmental committees and an environmental reporting system)

        ❏   An agreement between Zanussi and the FLM Union, also between Enichem and the FULC Union, envisaging joint consultative bodies concerning themselves, *inter alia*, with environmental matters.

Examples of Cooperative Environment Policy within the Context of Industrial Relations   **5/1**

ANNEX 5/2

W Z B   Ecologically extended Labour Policy Project

I   ☐   Local agreements on supervision and improvement of the environment, e.g. in Genoa and in Val Chiavenna, involving municipal governments, regional administrations, unions, employees' representations and environmental groups.

    ☐   A declared programme of reorganisation of the steel industry, signed by the government, the relevant regional administrations, companies involved and the unions

NL   ☐   National discussions within tripartite Economic and Social Council (SER)

    ☐   Agreement between the largest employers' association, VNO and the largest union, FNV, concerning ecological questions, in an attempt to set up working groups and a campaign under the heading "environmental protection within the company"

    ☐   Involvement of the unions in bilateral discussions between the government and industrial associations

    ☐   Collective agreements at industrial and company level which also include environmental-protection clauses (63 out of 161 agreements in 1991)

    ☐   Consultation rights, e.g. for works councils, within the framework of the "company environmental protection system"

Sp   ☐   Joint declaration by CC.OO business association and the UGT umbrella association concerning a concerted policy which will also include certain aspects of environmental protection

    ☐   Establishment of joint labour and environmental protection committees on the basis of the 7th Chemical Industry Agreement

UK   ☐   Proposal by umbrella trade-union council for a joint environmental policy within all companies, in the form of a "Model Green Agreement"

    ☐   Agreement between British Telecom and the NCU Union concerning joint environmental-protection initiatives

    ☐   Conduct of selected corporate "eco-audits" with union involvement

Examples of Cooperative Environment Policy within the Context of Industrial Relations

ANNEX 5/3

W Z B   Ecologically extended Labour Policy Project

UK   ☐   Extension of labour safety committee's duties to include environmental topics at Dunlop's

     ☐   Negotiations concerning waste disposal at SMS Chemicals, with participation of the shop stewards

---

Examples of Cooperative Environment Policy within the Context of Industrial Relations   **5/3**

European Foundation for the Improvement of Living and Working Conditions

Structures and trends in the greening of industrial relations in the countries of the EC

Luxembourg: Office for Official Publications of the European Community

1992—42 p.— 29.7 cm × 21.0 cm

ISBN 92-826-4958-X

Price (excluding VAT) in Luxembourg: ECU 6

Venta y suscripciones • Salg og abonnement • Verkauf und Abonnement • Πωλήσεις και συνδρομές
Sales and subscriptions • Vente et abonnements • Vendita e abbonamenti
Verkoop en abonnementen • Venda e assinaturas

BELGIQUE / BELGIË

**Moniteur belge /
Belgisch Staatsblad**
Rue de Louvain 42 / Leuvenseweg 42
1000 Bruxelles / 1000 Brussel
Tél. (02) 512 00 26
Fax 511 01 84
CCP / Postrekening 000-2005502-27

Autres distributeurs /
Overige verkooppunten

**Librairie européenne/
Europese Boekhandel**
Avenue Albert Jonnart 50 /
Albert Jonnartlaan 50
1200 Bruxelles / 1200 Brussel
Tél. (02) 734 02 81
Fax 735 08 60

Jean De Lannoy
Avenue du Roi 202 /Koningslaan 202
1060 Bruxelles / 1060 Brussel
Tél. (02) 538 51 69
Télex 63220 UNBOOK B
Fax (02) 538 08 41

CREDOC
Rue de la Montagne 34 / Bergstraat 34
Bte 11 / Bus 11
1000 Bruxelles / 1000 Brussel

DANMARK

**J. H. Schultz Information A/S
EF-Publikationer**
Ottiliavej 18
2500 Valby
Tlf. 36 44 22 66
Fax 36 44 01 41
Girokonto 6 00 08 86

BR DEUTSCHLAND

Bundesanzeiger Verlag
Breite Straße
Postfach 10 80 06
5000 Köln 1
Tel. (02 21) 20 29-0
Telex ANZEIGER BONN 8 882 595
Fax 20 29 278

GREECE/ΕΛΛΑΔΑ

G.C. Eleftheroudakis SA
International Bookstore
Nikis Street 4
10563 Athens
Tel. (01) 322 63 23
Telex 219410 ELEF
Fax 323 98 21

ESPAÑA

Boletín Oficial del Estado
Trafalgar, 27
28010 Madrid
Tel. (91) 44 82 135

Mundi-Prensa Libros, S.A.
Castelló, 37
28001 Madrid
Tel. (91) 431 33 99 (Libros)
431 32 22 (Suscripciones)
435 36 37 (Dirección)
Télex 49370-MPLI-E
Fax (91) 575 39 98

Sucursal:

Librería Internacional AEDOS
Consejo de Ciento, 391
08009 Barcelona
Tel. (93) 301 86 15
Fax (93) 317 01 41

**Llibreria de la Generalitat
de Catalunya**
Rambla dels Estudis, 118 (Palau Moja)
08002 Barcelona
Tel. (93) 302 68 35
302 64 62
Fax (93) 302 12 99

FRANCE

**Journal officiel
Service des publications
des Communautés européennes**
26, rue Desaix
75727 Paris Cedex 15
Tél. (1) 40 58 75 00
Fax (1) 40 58 75 74

IRELAND

Government Supplies Agency
4-5 Harcourt Road
Dublin 2
Tel. (1) 61 31 11
Fax (1) 78 06 45

ITALIA

Licosa Spa
Via Duca di Calabria, 1/1
Casella postale 552
50125 Firenze
Tel. (055) 64 54 15
Fax 64 12 57
Telex 570466 LICOSA I
CCP 343 509

GRAND-DUCHÉ DE LUXEMBOURG

Messageries Paul Kraus
11, rue Christophe Plantin
2339 Luxembourg
Tél. 499 88 88
Télex 2515
Fax 499 88 84 44
CCP 49242-63

NEDERLAND

SDU Overheidsinformatie
Externe Fondsen
Postbus 20014
2500 EA 's-Gravenhage
Tel. (070) 37 89 911
Fax (070) 34 75 778

PORTUGAL

Imprensa Nacional
Casa da Moeda, EP
Rua D. Francisco Manuel de Melo, 5
1092 Lisboa Codex
Tel. (01) 69 34 14

**Distribuidora de Livros
Bertrand, Ld.ª**
Grupo Bertrand, SA
Rua das Terras dos Vales, 4-A
Apartado 37
2700 Amadora Codex
Tel. (01) 49 59 050
Telex 15798 BERDIS
Fax 49 60 255

UNITED KINGDOM

HMSO Books (PC 16)
HMSO Publications Centre
51 Nine Elms Lane
London SW8 5DR
Tel. (071) 873 2000
Fax GP3 873 8463
Telex 29 71 138

ÖSTERREICH

**Manz'sche Verlags-
und Universitätsbuchhandlung**
Kohlmarkt 16
1014 Wien
Tel. (0222) 531 61-0
Telex 11 25 00 BOX A
Fax (0222) 531 61-39

SUOMI

Akateeminen Kirjakauppa
Keskuskatu 1
PO Box 128
00101 Helsinki
Tel. (0) 121 41
Fax (0) 121 44 41

NORGE

Narvesen information center
Bertrand Narvesens vei 2
PO Box 6125 Etterstad
0602 Oslo 6
Tel. (2) 57 33 00
Telex 79668 NIC N
Fax (2) 68 19 01

SVERIGE

BTJ
Box 200
22100 Lund
Tel. (046) 18 00 00
Fax (046) 18 01 25

SCHWEIZ / SUISSE / SVIZZERA

OSEC
Stampfenbachstraße 85
8035 Zürich
Tel. (01) 365 54 49
Fax (01) 365 54 11

CESKOSLOVENSKO

NIS
Havelkova 22
13000 Praha 3
Tel. (02) 235 84 46
Fax 42-2-264775

MAGYARORSZÁG

Euro-Info-Service
Budapest I. Kir.
Attila út 93
1012 Budapest
Tel. (1) 56 82 11
Telex (22) 4717 AGINF H-61
Fax (1) 17 59 031

POLSKA

Business Foundation
ul. Krucza 38/42
00-512 Warszawa
Tel. (22) 21 99 93, 628-28-82
International Fax&Phone
(0-39) 12-00-77

JUGOSLAVIJA

Privredni Vjesnik
Bulevar Lenjina 171/XIV
11070 Beograd
Tel. (11) 123 23 40

CYPRUS

**Cyprus Chamber of Commerce and
Industry**
Chamber Building
38 Grivas Dhigenis Ave
3 Deligiorgis Street
PO Box 1455
Nicosia
Tel. (2) 449500/462312
Fax (2) 458630

TÜRKIYE

**Pres Gazete Kitap Dergi
Pazarlama Dağitim Ticaret ve sanayi
AŞ**
Narlibahçe Sokak N. 15
Istanbul-Cağaloğlu
Tel. (1) 520 92 96 - 528 55 66
Fax 520 64 57
Telex 23822 DSVO-TR

CANADA

Renouf Publishing Co. Ltd
Mail orders — Head Office:
1294 Algoma Road
Ottawa, Ontario K1B 3W8
Tel. (613) 741 43 33
Fax (613) 741 54 39
Telex 0534783

Ottawa Store:
61 Sparks Street
Tel. (613) 238 89 85

Toronto Store:
211 Yonge Street
Tel. (416) 363 31 71

UNITED STATES OF AMERICA

UNIPUB
4611-F Assembly Drive
Lanham, MD 20706-4391
Tel. Toll Free (800) 274 4888
Fax (301) 459 0056

AUSTRALIA

Hunter Publications
58A Gipps Street
Collingwood
Victoria 3066

JAPAN

Kinokuniya Company Ltd
17-7 Shinjuku 3-Chome
Shinjuku-ku
Tokyo 160-91
Tel. (03) 3439-0121

Journal Department
PO Box 55 Chitose
Tokyo 156
Tel. (03) 3439-0124

AUTRES PAYS
OTHER COUNTRIES
ANDERE LÄNDER

**Office des publications officielles
des Communautés européennes**
2, rue Mercier
2985 Luxembourg
Tél. 49 92 81
Télex PUBOF LU 1324 b
Fax 48 85 73/48 68 17
CC bancaire BIL 8-109/6003/700

12/91

Bibliothèques
Université d'Ottawa
Échéance

Libraries
University of Ottawa
Date Due